The Weight She Carried

Shasta Mignon

Printed in the United States of America

First Printing, 2016

978-1-941749-69-2

LCCN 2017939015

4-P Publishing

Chattanooga, TN 37416

Book cover design by ronblache.com, Ronald Blache

Please visit my website for more information and resources. www.Shastamignon.com

Join our private Facebook community: **The Weight She Carried Together**. It's a place where members can connect, continue the discussion on the topics discussed in the book, as well get more information on upcoming events based off the book.

Acknowledgments

I'd like to make sure Chancy, knows that the sacrifices you have made for our family is golden, and for that, I say THANKS.

To Kyah, Kam, and Lala- This is all for you, my lifelines, the three of you give me three reasons to never give up and to keep fighting for more, so I can and will leave a legacy behind. When you look back over your childhood, you will realize I always had your best interests in mind and heart. I love you, and I am so proud of the ladies you will become. Thank you for challenging and allowing me to chase my dreams, so all of yours will be at your feet.

To my mother, Constance Yvonne, the road was hard and long but we stayed the course.

Ronald Blache, thanks for not blocking my many texts for favors. You are truly Heaven sent.

My aunts Calvereen, and Joyce you each showed me a woman's strength through life's ups and downs also my many aunts in Snowhill.

If I didn't mention you by name charge my head because you all know who you are and what you mean to me.

For Miss Louise Ervin without your encouragement and love, I might have given up on my dreams. You were also "So Proud of me." Thank you for everything but most importantly for being my mother's friend so that you could be my biggest cheerleader. Had it not been for you I hate to think where I'd be. You're truly my angel.

To the memory of the many strong women I lost along my journey, and to the glue that held my family together, my beautiful grandmother, Marion Williams, my aunts, Belinda, Cindy and Delphine, my godmother Dinky, LaTasha Todd, Micci, Lucky, LaKeisha Bonner-Coleston, Ashley Mckenzie, Glenda & Tyeshia Petite.

To James Reynolds, our walking dictionary, as the girls call you. Thank for being there when I needed advice like only you could give.

To my Daddy, James O. Bonner, in life you made me the ultimate daddy's girl. I wanted for nothing and you gave me everything. I know I didn't become a female drag racer, but I always wanted to make you proud.

To the memory of my big/little brother D'Angelo Marquis Vance, you were older but I always acted like the big bad wolf. I didn't play when it came to you, and we all knew it.

Every time I meet new people I find out that you played an important part in their lives that I never knew about. You were a father figure to many, an uncle, a mentor, and a gift to others that met you through your love for singing.

For anyone that helped, inspired, or listened to me say "this is what I wanted to do", I say Thank You.

Last, but not least, thank you, The Readers, for reading my book.

About the Author

Shasta was born and raised in Chattanooga, TN. She graduated from Tyner Academy High school. She attended Tennessee State University for a short period before returning to Chattanooga. She received her cosmetology license from Chattanooga State Community College. Shasta worked in insurance before returning to Chattanooga State to pursue a degree in Media Technology and finally began to discover the love for all things media.

Shasta has served as a mentor to youth in the community. During her free time, she enjoys spending time, with her children, acting, and having a good laugh.

Shasta is currently working to launch new media projects, related to *"The Weight She Carried" and more.*

Please visit the website for more information and resources at www.Shastamignon.com. Join the **secret** Facebook group *The Weight She Carried Together.*

Contact Shasta at
Phone 678-653-5135
Email Bossyshasta@gmail.com
Facebook Shasta Mignon
Twitter Bossyshasta
Instagram shastamignoninc

Foreword

Life stories...they free us. They bind us. They help us to relate to one another. I am honored to be asked to provide a few words for this amazing project because it is in telling our stories through poetry or any written word that we document them for others.

Writing down the work means this work becomes alive; a living thing. Whether readers buy it intentionally or stumble across its presence, they will lose themselves, find themselves, or release themselves to tell their own stories in whatever way it inspires them. It is far beyond the time for keeping the **secrets** that have forced us to be less than who we were designed to become. Those same **secrets** that have wicked out our potential of greatness like the cold, wet fingers of time and old age on our lives' fragrant candles. Yes, this work is overdue. This collec-tion will be the catalyst for so many who read it. It will inspire readers to move.

I read from its pages and related to its content on a very personal level. Congratulations, Shasta! You have collect-ed some of the finest, most delicate and transparent pieces of shattered feelings and woven them together to create a masterpiece. Some of your readers will turn these pages and be introduced to their truer selves... again. May they find kinship, healing, and forgiveness for themselves in these pages.

Linda Murray Bullard, MBA

Author of "The Well Ran Dry: Memoirs of a Motherless Child"

LSMB Business Solutions, LLC, Chattanooga, TN

Preface

As a black female growing up in the South, I have come in contact with plenty of women.

Globally throughout history, black women have been forced to be the backbone of the community. For instance, during slavery men were sold away from their families: wives and kids, so the women had no choice but to be the head of the household. We, as black women, are strong and made of something unlike this world. We make magic happen every day while there's a tornado going on inside of us, and no one will ever know the magnitude of the weight we carry daily. Why?

For so many years, we were taught that we can't show any signs of weakness because of our pride, or if we don't talk about it then nobody would know about it. This type of madness has caused a crack in our foundation. Our bodies were made to bring forth life yet we don't tell when someone is hurting us or when we need mental help. When I was growing up, Lifetime Movies were big, and we always thought that those movies were about and for women of other races, but they were about the women who were made to speak out, and say, "Yes, I was raped. Yes, I was molested. Yes, I was beaten. Yes, I need help."

I wrote "The Weight She Carried," because I began to see most of the women that look like me, and some that don't, face issues every day but we still have to keep going as if nothing is bothering us on the inside. I know plenty of women that are sick and tired of being sick and tired, but they have to keep moving without ceasing because we carry the weight of the world every day, but it gets heavy. Even the strongest woman needs a release but we don't want to appear weak or needy; there isn't room for both. In my own life, I can look back on times when I needed help, but my strong will wouldn't allow me to ask for it; I almost paid for it with my life. PRIDE is a killer, a silent killer.

This book was probably the easiest yet the hardest book to complete because these ladies literally were in my head demanding I tell their story, but they were no help with book title nor cover ideas. I pray if you recognize one or two of these women, you will extend a little kindness to your sisters. I pray this book causes us to start a conversation about who we know in our lives that might have been through some of these same issues, and we listen to their stories, at the very least.

Shasta

Contents

Little Girl Lost - Brittany

Forget the personal issues
When you been what I been through,
Hey if you believe it,
Then you could conceive it. ~ Jay-Z

Yeah, I talk loud!

So what, you may think you know my story, but you don't know me.

Behind my loud mouth, is a scared lil girl.

I don't and can't show.

See when I was eight my daddy died;

My mama couldn't handle it, so she checked out.

I was left to fend for myself; some days I ate some days I didn't.

Nobody told me about a period or puberty.

Nobody told me about a bird or a bee.

What was I to do?

When the first dude came along and said all the right things, I was screwed, pun intended.

I wasn't daddy's little girl or mama's baby,

So when he said I was a pretty thing and he loved me and would never hurt me,

I believed him and gave it up. Two months later that nigga was gone.

Oh, he wasn't the last; their faces changed but the game was all too familiar.

But hell I didn't know I was being used.

They bought me some clothes, a few pieces of cheap jewelry, and they fed me so I thought that was love.

By seventeen I had a baby, two miscarriages, and a few STDs.

I've been raped, beaten, abused and used.

I didn't love myself 'cause I never knew true love.

To all these niggas I was just property to be owned and traded.

I was drinking and getting high to cover up my pain

The higher I got the better I felt; I was numb.

I just didn't care about nothing or nobody.

Cause ain't nobody ever cared for me.

I wasn't daddy's little girl or mama's baby.

I barely finished high school working fast-food and pregnant again by a different guy.

My grandmamma was raising my first baby but wouldn't take this one.

I'd probably be dead if it weren't for my grandmamma.

She was as mean as a snake, but the heart of an angel.

"Your fast ass living too fast," is what she used to say.

I'd show up at her door, many times battered and bruised; she would clean me up and nurse me back to health, then off I would go back into my world of hell.

She died when I was twenty-four; that's the first time I'd ever stepped foot in anybody's church, but it felt like home.

That's when it hit me.

If I were the loudest person in the room, no one would know about my past.

No one would suspect that I was damaged goods and would never be anyone's wife.

I once heard some church folks say everybody has a past, but is everybody as good at hiding theirs, as I am?

Hell no!

When I talk loud and shift my eyes away it's my way of covering up my scars.

Until you know me don't judge the way I live my life.

Never Judge a Book by Its Dress-
Queenie

Girlfriend, let me break it down for you again
You know I only say it 'cause I'm truly genuine
Don't be a hard rock when you're really a gem
~Lauryn Hill

I've slept with a lot of men.

Does that make me a hoe?

It just means I know how to enjoy myself.

I go out and make things happen.

Oh, but you church folk so quick to judge me like you never have sex.

Besides sex is normal, we all do it.

It's your way of thinking that makes it nasty.

I love men, and hell I love sex when it's done right.

I protect myself all the time; I carry my own protection.

I don't fall for that "I'm clean" stuff.

I ain't stupid my home girl got HIV from a clean dude.

Sad part about it is, she got it from her husband of eleven years.

I love myself too much to go out like that.

Plus, men have been sleeping around since Adam, talking about he was a player.

You church women look down your noses at me.

I'm a grown confident woman while you talk about me behind my back "Whore. Slut. Freak. Bitch."

Everything but the name my mama gave me when she pushed me out, Queenie.

My name and this letter was all she gave me.

Dear Queenie,

I gave you this name so that people would have to call you a Queen and treat you like royalty. I know you'll probably think I am selfish for leaving you, but it isn't that effortless. I loved you from the minute I heard your little heartbeat.

I wasn't supposed to get pregnant, but I loved your dad and knew he would want to be a family. I was wrong, and my family didn't want me to throw my life away on a guy that didn't love me enough to claim our baby. He wanted something different out of life; I guess I wasn't it.

I figure if I leave you then someone may give you the kind of life you deserve. It's gone be a lot of stuff said about me, but please don't believe it.

I made sure to read every book I could get my hands on about a healthy pregnancy, and I followed it to a tee.

Your dad gave me $575 to get rid of you and I thought about it, but I couldn't go through with it. I made the appointment, I went to the clinic, but I just couldn't get out the car; the protestors out front and my own conscience frightened me.

Please understand I am seventeen, afraid and alone. I am in love with a black man, and my parents are old fashioned when it comes to race and being in the south with closed-minded people doesn't help.

*I will always love you, my beautiful black Queen,
and when you're ready to come looking for me. I'll be
here.*

Love,

Your mom,

Jessica.

And just like that my life was forever altered.

I thank God my dad's mom, Nita, came and got me;
she raised me.

I think the only reason why was because she had all
boys and really wanted a girl.

Even though I looked just like my mother, whom
she hated and referred to as that white junky heifer
who tried to ruin her son's life.

My dad was her youngest and her favorite; she was
overprotective of him.

My uncles were wild and reckless; they stayed in
and out of jail.

They always ended up at our house.

She was determined for me to have a better life.

Nita made sure I didn't step out the house looking
any less than stunning.

My grandma made sure that I learned proper
hygiene at a young age.

She said white people smelled like wet dog when
they sweat or get wet.

I just figured it was another one of her silly Old wives' tales, that she would throw out at me randomly, like "don't ever sit your purse on the floor cause your money would be low, or a fish dream means somebody in the family is pregnant."

She messed up my curly hair because she hadn't ever had to do "mixed hair."

She always put it in a messy ponytail slicked up with blue grease.

I was made fun of in school because of my pale complexion and wild hair.

My dad left me, moved across town, and made a family with his third baby mama.

His last baby mama was evil and wouldn't allow me to be a part of their lives.

She hated me because I was mixed and his only daughter.

His baby mama treated me as if I was invisible.

My grandmother would always say she didn't trust her.

She told my dad to be sure he always watched me and protected me when she passed away.

I was 13 but she made him promise to raise me right.

She left him her house and made him her benefactor for my life not to be so disastrous.

My daddy didn't really keep women around too long, so I never had a steady female in my life.

A teacher at school taught me about using pads and making sure I had them.

I don't know what I would've done without Miss Miles.

She told me I was smart, and she knew I would be successful at whatever I attempted.

 She kept up with me, made sure I applied, and got accepted into college.

I couldn't get out my daddy's house fast enough.

He worked a lot and made sure I had what I needed, but he didn't spend time with me nor was he involved in my life.

He just took care of me.

I wouldn't even know what is love had it not been for my Grandma Nita and Miss Miles.

I can't blame my past on what I am now.

Once I got to high school, I realized the power I possessed with a snap of my fingers.

 The boys flocked and I hadn't even started having sex with yet.

My grandma taught me better than that, but I let them get to third base to get what I wanted or needed.

In college, that's where it all changed.

It was so refreshing being on my own for the first time and making my own decisions.

I was glad not feeling like an intruder in someone else's space, or having to walk on eggshells.

But I ain't gone front, I'm human and I hurt too.

No, I don't like it but this is the hand I was dealt.

It's women like you that make me not even want to step foot in any church.

I was raised in the church.

I refuse to change who I am because of your insecurities.

Maybe if you would loosen up some then your men wouldn't be giving me the side eye.

Bet you would be mad if you knew that's the reason I put an extra sway in my hips.

I mean dang, we are all there for the same reasons yet you act as though my sins are worse than your sins.

Aren't we all there searching for forgiveness and to repent our sins?

Doesn't the Bible say, "Judge not, that ye be not judged?"

I never said I sleep with every man I meet.

I try to avoid the married ones, ones with families, wives, or girlfriends.

Of course, sometimes they lie but don't you worry I always send him right on back to you.

A lot of you should be thanking me for saving your broken relationships because after the sex I'm done anyways.

I ain't trying to fall in love with them.

Why on earth would I want your man, so he can put me in your shoes and cheat on me?

Ha, I think not; that ain't me 'cause I ain't that monogamous marriage type.

I just have a need to fulfill an itch that needs scratching.

Yet you judge me but what about him?

It takes two to tango, and what if I wasn't aware of his deceit?

I don't throw rocks and hide my hands.

I go into every situation with a clear mind.

Men who sleep around with lots of beautiful women get patted on the back.

Women, we get branded with the "Scarlett Letter."

If we wear red lipstick, red dresses, or red shoes and we're tramps.

Red just happens to compliment my light complexion.

For the record, yes, I love sex and I ain't gone apologize for it.

I work, pay my taxes, and I'm a law-abiding citizen.

However, on the weekend I'm letting my hair down, putting on a tight red outfit, and the baddest heels I can find.

Hell I just wanna have some fun.

Plus, I paid good money for my ass and tits trying to have a body like Beyonce, why would I hide them?

Please don't be intimidated by my beauty.

I'm just a lady that happens to wear red.

Next time, just slide over and let a bitch sit down.

Chances are we may be closer than you think.

Stop hating me long enough to learn a thing or two on how to keep your man happy at home.

Smooches

What the Eyes Can't See-
Tabitha

*It's been too hard living, but I'm afraid to die
'Cause I don't know what's up there, beyond
the sky It's been a long, a long time coming ~
Sam Cook*

I always seem to blend into the background;

I go unnoticed.

I'm not the pretty one;

I'm not the sexy.

I'm just average.

I'm existing.

Yeah, I get lonely at times.

I can't help that I tend to push people away.

You see, under my long sleeves and pants are my hidden **secrets**.

Secrets that should never be revealed.

No one would understand my pain.

Since my high school years, I've carried this **secret**.

It started off as something I'd occasionally do.

It quickly snowballed out of control.

I make small slashes to release some of my inner pain.

It's not that bad, so don't look at me like that

See, that's exactly why I didn't want to expose myself 'cause I knew you would go right to judging me.

You can't judge me because you don't know me.

I am hurting on the inside until it all became too much.

It's the only way I know how to cope was to see the pain bleed out.

You try walking in my shoes and I'm sure you'll find a way to cope too.

At least I ain't strung out on drugs or whoring around.

It was hell growing up in my house.

I have been through a lot of shit.

My mama tried to be a good mother, but hell she fell short many times.

She had three kids I was the oldest and my sister and brother were twins.

She was married three times by the time I left for college, and on the hunt to land number four.

Husband number one went to jail for selling drugs to an undercover cop and murdering him trying to get away.

He was my daddy.

Mama found out she was pregnant two days after he was sentenced to life in prison.

I've never met nor talked to the man.

Freddy was the second husband and he was the twins' father and the worst one.

Mama was working and going to school at night, so we were often left alone with Freddy.

It didn't take long for him to come after me.

Started out just making gestures then he changed to mind games.

I was good when my mama was home but he told lies on me so she would punish me.

I was only ten, young and innocent, still able to see some good in this world.

He would walk in on me coming out the tub, and when I would try to cover my body he would move my hands away.

One night he said he had to check in between my legs to make sure no boys had tried to test out the product.

He made me lay back on their bed while he used his two fingers to inspect me.

It hurt which made him smile "Yeah, see that means I'll be able to break you in, so you'll be ripe for the next man."

My mother was clueless about the whole everything.

She allowed Freddy to discipline us and he enjoyed it all too well.

I was punished for the bad things the twins had done, which I took just so he wouldn't go after my little sister.

The night I wished would never happen came and I wasn't sleeping either.

I was actually expecting him because I knew this nightmare was coming, but nothing would have ever prepared me for the hell I was about to live.

Tears immediately formed in my eyes

He turned the light on, walked over to my bed, and climbed in beside me.

He started rubbing on my back and squeezing my new forming breast.

His hands were rough, and so was he.

His breath reeked of alcohol, as he licked my ears while he touched himself moaning and whispering,

"Daddy's here to make it all better, but remember it's our **secret** because your mama wouldn't like that you make me happy."

I started crying harder and closed my eyes really tight; that seem to excite him more.

He climbed on top of me, and I felt as though his weight would crush me.

He parted my legs and rubbed himself on my innocence, and tore through my youth.

He broke my hymen and my future.

I felt my hopefulness spill down my legs.

I stopped feeling everything at that moment.

I went numb and completely shut down, forever.

Even to this day, I'm numb to feelings.

I'd seen the puppet shows about good and bad touches urging me to tell an adult.

For some reason, I couldn't open my mouth to tell anyone that something bad was happening to me.

This happened weekly over the next three years.

I became afraid of the dark and was terrified for my mother to leave me behind.

I was wetting the bed, and I became very nervous and had panic attacks.

My teacher called one day to tell my mother that I was failing school and seem withdrawn.

It was a red flag she wanted to talk to my mama before things got too bad, and she would have to report it.

My mom finally questioned what had gotten into me because she still had no clue of the hell I had endured.

She never noticed that half my damn hair was falling out nor that I pulled out the other half.

I told her what Freddy had done to me.

She apologized and admitted it had happened to her when she was young.

I was afraid she wouldn't believe, but she did and put him out the house.

She made it very clear that we needed to keep this to ourselves, just like her mother made them do after her uncle molested her and her sister.

Nobody could've prepared me for the massive weight she was asking me to carry with this **secret.**

It was too much to ask of a small child, and it took its toll on me.

I think I need medications for my nerves.

Things were hard, but we were close for a while.

Until she got lonely and found husband number three but this time, she had finally found a good guy.

She explained to him how Freddy hurt me, and he said he would never do that.

He was a real dad because he had two daughters of his own that he loved and cared about.

He made us a family finally and we took vacations and went on outings together.

It took a few years for me to get used to a man not looking at me for his own pleasure.

I was getting used to having a daddy.

BAM!

He had a heart attack at work.

He was gone no warning or nothing.

I was devastated, and that's when it began.

If I hurt, I slashed.

I was tired of crying.

I was all cried out, so instead I cut to feel better.

It was like a release of some sort.

When my blood ran down my body it freed my pain.

The marks tripled over the years, but the twins were the only ones to notice.

They learned over the years to keep many **secrets**.

I knew they wouldn't tell anyone.

I graduated to my legs in my junior year.

My mama was too busy trying to live her life to even notice my pain, my awkward puberty years, or me.

It was as though I was invisible to her like if she dealt with my rape, and me she would have to confront her own rape;

I don't think she could handle it because she was made to bury her pain, so that's how she wanted me to get through mine.

I never understood how black families were raised to sweep issues under the rug, hoping they would go away without ever seeking help.

I never stopped cutting.

I'm a successful manager at my company that has no personal life, no boyfriend, and no fun.

I do, however, have lots of batteries.

I won't get close to anyone that might expose my **secrets**.

Don't mind me.

I'm busy climbing the corporate ladder to the top.

I'm staying away from love, hurt, and pain.

I just exist.

It's the only way I know how to protect my sanity and myself.

I go to counseling, and I pop the occasional Xanax from time to time.

I sleep with a TV on, and I have a gun beside my bed and in every room in my house.

I promise I'll never be a sitting victim again.

My Man Was My Everything- Mercy

Besides the kids, I have nothing to show, wasted my years, a fool of a wife. I should've left your ass a long time ago ~Mary J. Blige

You think I got it made huh, with nice clothes, hair, nails, and the decent car?

Oh, and don't forget the adoring husband waiting at home in the large house with four great kids.

I got a little money and the picture-perfect life.

It makes you kind of envious; you want my life.

What you don't know is: it's all a front.

My husband, the pastor, makes my life a living hell Monday through Saturday.

Yet every Sunday I sit in the front pew as if I don't have a care in the world.

He provides a great lifestyle, but the price the kids and I pay is too high.

He makes my kids go to a very selective private school, where they are minorities.

It's only for the elite spenders, and he sits on the school board since he donates money to the school.

I hate it and my children hate it.

Even though we fit in financially, they still look at us as if we don't belong.

Oh, but they love his dirty drawers.

At home it's a war zone; we walk around on eggshells, never sure what kind of mood he's in because he runs hot and cold.

Even as large as our house is, there still isn't enough room to run from his wrath.

He's such a hypocrite, the devil disguised in a suit.

Every word that comes out his mouth on Sunday mornings is a lie.

He's an adulterer, a liar, and a cheater.

He is verbally and physically abusive towards the kids and me.

Members of the church have no idea that the leader of their flock is going to bust hell wide open.

He sleeps with women in the church, married, single, it doesn't matter to him.

I always know when he's having an affair because we don't have sex during those times.

I guess he's not man enough for that much sex, which is fine with me.

We've had sex 643 times throughout our 13-year long marriage.

Oh yeah, I keep up and write it down.

It's the worst sex I've ever had since I started at age 19.

I have to use my vibrator to finish myself off or fake until he gets his.

I guess he thinks it's sympathy sex, but I wish he would just have outside affairs and not bother me for boring sex.

I could probably win an award for the acting I do in bed with Pastor.

I've been told he has a preference of high yellow women with big thighs, which was new to me because I'm neither one of those.

I think he preyed upon me because of my insecurities.

There's no way I could've passed the brown paper sack test.

My skin is the color of caramel toffee.

I'm tall and skinny, well I was before I started having his babies.

Pastor Brooks was good at keeping his "what's done in the dark," business quiet.

Until he got jammed up, one of the deacons called me looking for his wife.

He thought we were lunching together.

My husband told me this same deacon was with him at the hospital praying with a dying church member.

It didn't take a rock scientist to realize they were together.

I saw the hotel charges on our personal account.

If he used the church's account it would've raised some eyebrows especially since said deacon was on the financial board.

The whispering started and people would become silent when I entered rooms.

I was the first lady so they still showed me some respect.

Two years later his dirty deeds came to light when he got one of his mistresses pregnant, and she wouldn't get rid of it.

I remember when the young girl came to the church under watch care while away from home.

I was one of her mentors while she was here going to college.

They made a fool of me.

Pastor Brooks made it clear to me that he wasn't going to lose his family or his church.

We went on pretending to be the happy Brooks' family.

I packed so many bags over the years to leave him, and then I realized I never could.

I decided to have a few affairs of my own.

It started out small but then I got so addicted to outside relationships.

I forgot to tend to home first.

I was so comfortable fooling around.

I started letting my side dudes come by the house when Pastor Brooks was out of town and my babies were in school.

That was until Pastor came home, I slipped.

I didn't check his calendar.

I was busted with my hand in the cookie jar, literally.

I put up with his affairs, his outside children, and the abuse, but I wasn't prepared for this.

He pulled out a gun on my lover and I.

He didn't put it away until he embarrassed and degraded me by making me please my boyfriend in front of him.

He took pictures and threatened to show them at church and to our kids if I didn't end it.

That's when the beatings became more severe.

He started hitting me in places that wouldn't be seen under my clothes.

I swear I've thought of at least a hundred of ways to kill him.

I had come to the conclusion that I would poison him.

I'm not a killer.

Besides I wouldn't want to leave my kids like that, so I became the world's best actress pretending to be a great 'First Lady'.

I was so good at faking orgasms and then going to the bathroom to really get the job done.

I was puzzled at what the outside chick was in it for 'cause it wasn't the sex, it was awful

She had to be in it for the church's money or status.

He was getting some type of prescription every month, which I'm assuming is Viagra since I'm not allowed to check our mailbox.

The very next sermon he preached about committing adultery made me vomit in my mouth.

I had to excuse myself from the front row.

I literally became ill from just looking at Pastor Brooks.

I stop going to church altogether.

I refused to be paraded around as a fraud with him that was the ultimate disrespect.

After the second month of missing church, he beat me like I was a stranger that spit in his face off the street.

My oldest son jumped on his back to stop the blows, and Pastor Brooks pushed my son so hard he fell back.

While he was standing over my son, delivering blows to our son, it gave me enough time to go get the same gun that bastard pulled on me.

Right before he reached down to strike my son, I fired a warning shot right above his head.

I could barely stand up.

"I want you to lay another finger on my child and the next warning shot will be between your twisted ass eyes!

Did you forget I wasn't always your first lady?

Now, I don't know if you believe all that bullshit you call yourself preaching about or not.

If you do then you must be ready to meet the God you been praying to all these years.

If not, I'd advise you to step away from my son and get the hell outta this house".

He took one step in my direction but seeing the death gaze my swollen eyes held he knew I was not to be tested, so he turned and walked away.

I called the police, had a restraining order filed, then I filed for divorce.

Before the ink dried on the decree, he had moved on with the college girl that had his youngest kid.

I was finally at the point where I could do me.

I took my kids out those private schools.

I put my house on the market below cost so it would sell quicker.

I pulled a whole "Waiting to Exhale" getting rid of his stuff.

I sold the valuable things and donated the other crap to the nearest homeless shelter.

I promised myself I would never allow a man to dictate who I was and what I could or would not do with my life.

I enrolled in school and got a job at a local daycare, finally, I was the Mercy I always wanted to be.

At forty-three, I was just now learning to be independent and do things for myself.

Pastor Brooks handled all the money and bills.

I had to learn how to pay bills and open a bank account.

I had to learn how to be a grown woman and handle my own business.

One thing I know for sure is, now that I've tasted this freedom.

I could never go back into another church or relationship like the one I came from.

Monster in My Closet-Charla

Whatever, don't kill, you make you stronger
Well, I must be the world's strongest woman
~Monica

I try to be as normal as I can be, but I have flashbacks and nightmares almost thirty years later; it affects my everyday life.

I have panic attacks, and I fear that my own children could fall prey to the same kind of havoc.

I know you're looking at me and you don't see any scars or deformities.

It makes you' wonder what on earth could cause this type of strife.

Oh no, I get it.

I have family members that don't understand why I don't come around.

Why I couldn't maintain a stable relationship.

You sure you want to know?

It all started when I was just six years old.

Raised by a single mother who had three other boys and no child support and she had to work.

I'm the second kid and there aren't more than 22 months between either of us.

By the time my mom was 24, she had four kids and a high school diploma.

She would find jobs, but they didn't pay enough for her to be able to take care of all of our needs and hers.

Yes, we were on food stamps, Section 8 and any other government assistance we could get.

She tried to at least make ends meet.

She pulled a few scams, ran lottery, let a few dudes sell drugs out the back of our house.

She never really hugged us or showed a lot of affection.

She did tell us that she loved us or she wouldn't have given up her life to raising us.

When she didn't have to work on the weekends, she liked to run the streets, just like all young women her age.

She could never afford a real sitter, so she left us with her nephew, the monster.

He didn't start off as a monster, but that's how it ended.

I was playing with one of my little brothers and I pushed him too hard, and he fell and started crying.

The Monster got up to see what was wrong.

I remember the whole room changed; it was hot and red.

The Monster's grin was evil as he realized my brother was telling on me.

I was so scared that I was going to get a whopping.

I didn't.

I ended up getting something much worse.

He said to apologize and hug him.

I went to hug my brother, but he stopped me and forced me to hug him instead.

I felt the bulge in his pants but knew nothing about it.

I did as I was told because I thought, "well this is better than a spanking."

The Monster told my brothers to go to bed, but I that I could stay up and watch TV with him in my mother's room.

I stuck out my tongue at my little brothers.

They all had a look of terror plastered on their faces as they walked away.

My oldest brother came running down the hall saying that our Mama wouldn't want me in her room if she wasn't there and I needed to go to my own room.

I thought he was jealous but he was trying to save me.

The Monster told my oldest brother to mind his damn business.

He pushed me towards my mom's bed and slammed the door in my brother's face.

He picked me up and placed me on the bed.

He turned on the TV and placed a VHS tape in the recorder and turned the light off.

The TV displayed a couple engaging in a sex act.

I had never seen this before but knew I wasn't supposed to be watching it.

The Monster slid his pants down and I closed my eyes because I knew I wasn't supposed to look at boys' private parts.

I felt the bed sink under his weight, and he was laying right next to me without clothes on.

I felt him taking my pants off, and I shook from the chill in the room.

I was so cold.

He began to lick on my neck and down to my bare non-formed breasts.

He forced me lick him, and when I didn't he hit me.

I was so scared and I cried out for my mama, but she wasn't there, nobody came for me.

He put his hand over my mouth and told me to stop screaming because nobody would help me.

No one would believe me because I was the bad girl.

Besides he was punishing me for pushing my brother.

There I was a six-year-old baby licking on a teenage boy that was damn near grown like they were doing on TV.

I guess I wasn't doing it right because he got mad and made me stop, and told me just to lay down and be still.

He stuck his finger in my "cookie," as my aunt called the vagina, and it immediately caused me to flinch in agony.

I cried out, "Ouch that hurts, please stop," with hot tears drenching my face.

He pushed me back and said it hurt because I wouldn't relax.

He said I was going to start liking it like the pretty lady on TV likes it.

I must have died at least twice that night because when he climbed on top of me and forced his penis inside my tight vagina.

All I could do is swarm in pain as he used his strength to hold me down, and I blacked out.

I stared into his face wanting him to die in that very moment as he thrust in and out of me.

I felt as though an eighteen-wheeler was tearing through my body.

He smiled and questioned, "Don't you want me?"

He was enjoying himself.

After he was done with me, I was sticky with blood and I had no idea what else.

He told me to get up and go bathe.

I was aching from pain with each step.

He told my oldest brother to make sure I took a bath.

"You better not say nothin' to yo mama, neither of you or next time it'll be a whole lot worse for you both," he warned.

The water was hot and felt as though it would burn my skin, and I wished for that distraction.

I'll never forget the aching soreness I carry with me today every time I have sex.

I wished for death to come for me.

I wanted to die so that I would never feel that type of pain again.

How did my mother come home and not notice a change in her only girl?

There was blood on the tissue when I wiped for 3 days.

"Mama, what does it mean when you have blood in your panties," I asked her?

She just brushed it off as if I was asking her questions about something I saw on TV.

She answered, "you'll get your period one day and you'll be able to have crumb snatching kids of your own."

He continued to molest me over the next four years.

But I suspect I wasn't the only one.

On the days he didn't come after me, I think he was molesting my brothers.

My Cabbage Patch dolls had holes in between their legs where he was molesting them too.

My mother was still clueless about the type of horrors that were taken place in her own house.

My mama just wanted to live and recapture her youth.

My mama was oblivious to the hell we were living in.

She was looking for a husband to take care of her and hopefully accept us as his own.

I think the monster finally left us alone because he had a steady girlfriend that he was sleeping with.

We found out later that she was pregnant.

I was relieved but it was short lived.

The monster was not only a child molester, but he was also evil as hell and couldn't get along with his parents, and they put him out of their house.

He was grown now and should have been able to afford his own place.

He couldn't keep a job because he was always drinking and smoking weed.

I didn't know he had moved into my grandmother's house.

Until one day, I had to ride the bus over there because my mother had company and my brother's had after school activities.

My grandmother always left an extra key under the flowerpot for the grandkids, so I let myself in, thinking I was alone.

I always hated using the restroom at school, so I ran straight to my grandmother's bathroom in her bedroom.

After washing my hands, I walked out of the room and bumped right into the Monster, and he smirked.

I felt the hairs on the back of my neck stand.

I was a twelve now, and tired of being scared.

I pushed past him and went into the kitchen.

He grabbed me from behind and threw me down on the floor pinning my arms back.

He placed his mouth on my left breast and growled, "Look, it fits my mouth like a glove."

I shoved him off and ran to the kitchen to grab a knife.

I screamed, "I will stick this shit in your eye and leave you bleeding on Granny's carpet. Fuck with me again. I've had enough.

I'm not scared of you anymore. I won't let you hurt me anymore."

At that moment, I meant every word I said out of my preteen mouth.

I threw the knife on the floor, grabbed my book bag, and stormed out the front door.

I went to neighbor's house until my oldest brother came to pick me up.

Over the next six years, I became very violent.

I fought every boy in the neighborhood.

I had a murderous mentally.

I'd never be hurt again.

I could easily be set off and everybody said, "Oh she's just hateful".

Nobody ever questioned why.

I needed someone to show me love and attention, and my mama was too busy with church, work, or with her new husband.

By age sixteen, the first boy to come along and say all those things I longed to hear, talked me right out my princess panties.

I gave up my virginity this time for real 'cause Tre said he loved me and he bought me a few cheap gifts.

I was hooked, line and sinker.

I did whatever I needed to do to be with him.

I snuck him in our house, and I snuck out to be with him, I skipped school, and I fought girls over him.

I stole money from my parents to buy him gifts, in hopes of buying his attention as well.

Over the next year, he treated me like crap, but I loved his dirty drawers.

By seventeen, I was pregnant.

My mama found out and made me have an abortion because she didn't want me to embarrass her in front of the church folks or our family.

She made him pay for half of the abortion and told everyone we were going prom dress shopping and having a girl's weekend getaway.

I remember seeing the protesters outside the clinic and wanting one of them to rescue me.

I walked in and saw so many girls.

I went into the exam room that was white and sterile and chills ran over my body.

I wanted to yell no and run out, but I knew my mama wouldn't let me leave the clinic with my baby still in my body.

I climbed on the cold table praying to God that my mother would have a change of heart and come racing through that door to stop the procedure.

It never happened.

I just knew if I had that baby, I'd finally have someone that would love me unconditionally, and the three of us could be a real family.

The doctor's eyes were a blur and I slowly crept into unconsciousness, but not without a fight.

Since the molestation, I never went to sleep hard because the Monster would come after me in my bed at night while I was asleep.

When the procedure was over, I was given juice, pain pills, and instructions on what to do and not do for the next four to six weeks.

I recovered in a hotel and went back to school two days later.

However, my boyfriend, Tre, didn't want anything to do with me because I killed his baby, which he didn't even want.

That night, I took one too many of those pills to give me rest, so I wouldn't feel the pain of yet another heartbreak.

Thank God nothing happened to my dumb ass.

I had to go on like everything was fine.

After months, I was finally able to move on.

Tre interfered with every relationship I attempted by spreading vicious lies about me.

He didn't want me but didn't want me to be with anyone else either.

I became reckless with my safety.

I didn't care whether I lived or died.

I ran with all the bad girls.

I was never in a gang but I hung with the gang banging girls and their dangerous boyfriends.

I witnessed some things I shouldn't have.

They say most girls become promiscuous and sleep around with a bunch of different guys after being molested, as a coping mechanism.

I didn't I just shut down and bottled up all my emotions.

Sex has never been pleasurable for me; it's more like a chore done to please a loved one.

I was stressed out with worry and fear.

My stepdad said something to me one day that triggered a bottled up emotion about what the Monster had done to me, and I blew up telling him, 'I wasn't gone to be molested again'.

That's how my parents found out.

Of course, the Monster denied it and called me a liar.

His mother said maybe it was one of my mother's old boyfriends and I'm just mistaken because I've always been fast and hot.

This immediately broke up our family.

My grades dropped, and I was depressed, which was unheard of in black families.

My mom said, "I just needed to go to church and have them pray for me at the altar."

My brothers denied anything had ever happened to us.

I guess they were too old to go through those painful past memories.

My stepdad assured me that no one else would ever hurt me again, as long as he was around.

That only lasted another year, he left when he caught my mother cheating with a deacon from her church.

I had to be strong for my younger brothers because our mother was hanging out even more she looking for a good man.

Our car was repossessed, and we had to move from our house into a small apartment.

I overheard my aunts saying that my mama gave all her money to that church.

At this point, I was damn near raising myself.

I woke up, got ready for school, came home, did chores and homework, and I worked.

I had my own money to get my hair and nails fixed.

I bought my own hygiene products and school clothes.

I had to give my mama money for living under "her roof" just like my oldest brother did because times were tough.

The summer before my senior year, my mama told me "I was wasting my time because my fast ass wouldn't graduate anyway, and if it weren't for her getting rid of my bastard baby and putting me on birth control I'd be a teen mom dropout."

I don't know why she said those things to me because through everything, I have kept my nose in a book.

Just by her saying that foul crap to me, I was determined to finish not just high school but college also.

My mother decided she was tired of working and needed to find a hustler husband to take care of her, and that's when she hooked back up with my oldest brother's dad.

My oldest brother was serving time for armed robbery, and they rekindled their love while visiting him.

I graduated from high school, and my own mother was not even in the audience.

She had something more important to take care of, with my oldest brother trying to get paroled.

My younger brothers went to live with their dad; I was stuck living with a lady that I didn't really know.

It was like she disliked me for looking like or sounding like my father, whoever he was.

I was the one she didn't want to love or have, despite her always saying I'm just like her.

I'm nothing like her now or ever.

She was never like a mother to me, more like a nanny made to raise me.

I sometimes question if I was adopted.

She acts as though she isn't my mom.

I'm still waiting on the **secret** to come out that she's really my aunt or cousin.

I went away to college on scholarships.

 I promised I was never going back to live with my mother.

I became a school counselor hoping to help kids like my younger self.

Finally, after kissing a lot of frogs, I met my Prince Charming.

He's the most wonderful man.

I told him about my sordid past and he loves me past my pains.

We got married when I realized that he knew everything about me and didn't judge me nor run off.

My husband and I have a wonderful son and beautiful daughter.

I finally let my mother back into my life after family counseling.

She tries to be a better grandmother than mother.

I see her efforts, but a part of me still blames her for not knowing that we were being hurt right under her nose and she didn't know.

My heart forgives her but my head won't let me forget.

At times, I remind her that she wasn't the greatest mother and to never meddle with the way I raise my kids.

I've never asked her for any advice, anyway.

I never will.

I will admit I am good at hiding my true feelings.

As a mother, I think you can sense a change in your children.

I couldn't imagine bringing kids into the world and allowing them to be hurt.

I sympathize with how some mothers would rather kill their kids than allow them to be hurt or suffer by this cruel world.

I vowed to my kids that I wouldn't allow them to be hurt the way my brothers and I were hurt.

I plan to tell my kids about my past so they will understand the reasons for my anxious and paranoid behavior as soon as they are old enough to handle it.

My babies are my whole world, and I never allow them away from me for too long.

They can't go to any sleep over's, and absolutely no out of town trips without me.

My mother-in-law was the only person I trust with my kids, and now my mother once she apologized and started counseling.

Yes, I've been called a helicopter mom.

If you looked at us you'd think we had the perfect family but behind closed doors things are different.

Prince Charming and I sleep in separate rooms.

I practically, sleep in our children's room;

I want to make sure they are safe.

I hardly sleep though because I watch my children sleeping at night.

I check and recheck doors and windows to make sure everything is locked and secured.

I'm so obsessive because I'll be damned if I sit around and allow my kids to go through what I went through.

Sometimes, I watch my husband sleep.

I wonder what he's dreaming about.

I wonder if he fantasizes about other women 'cause I know there must be a better wife out there for him.

He needs a wife who isn't damaged goods.

He needs a woman who will please him sexually, or at least one who doesn't cringe when he touches her.

I love him, I really do, but I have flashbacks of the Monster violating me.

I can't fully relax and enjoy myself during sex.

I tense up causing pain to my vaginal muscles.

It hurts so bad that I always run to the shower immediately after to clean myself and cry alone.

 It feels like rape all over again and I feel dirty.

I have night terrors, and when he tries to comfort me, I end up swinging at him.

He's so patient and understanding with me, which is why I know he deserves someone better.

I refuse to go back to counseling.

The first time I tried counseling was during college, but the doctor couldn't fix me.

I refused the Zoloft she offered.

I wasn't crazy.

I didn't need pills.

I walked away and never looked back.

I know I have posttraumatic stress disorder.

Sometimes, I just don't want to get out of bed.

Some days I can't eat, and other days I eat too much.

I want to love.

I want be in love with my perfect Prince Charming.

I can't because I'm not whole.

I can't please him sexually because I associate sex with filth and pain and not the beautiful act between a man and his wife.

I cannot show affections the way a female should, not to my husband, my kids, nor my mother.

I don't like to be touched.

I take at least two showers a day.

I never feel clean.

I wish there were a magic pill that would fix, me but there isn't.

I pray God fixes me before I lose my husband and my mind.

I thank God I don't look like what I'm going through.

I still see the Monster.

I know he sees me.

He thinks I'm still that weak six-year-old he tried to destroy.

That scared little girl died in my mother's bed the first night he violated me.

She was replaced with a cold detached shell of a person with a homicidal mama bear that could snap at any moment.

I have thought of a million ways to kill him.

I know it's better for me to act as though he's dead to me.

I dare him to utter a word in my direction; if he does he's dead on site.

My Prince told me to say the word, and he'll put a price on his head to have him killed.

I know our kids need us; I always say no, but I really do want him dead for what he took from my brothers and me.

I want the Monster to suffer a slow painful death for what he did to us.

I found out my brothers and I weren't his only victims.

I always heard karma is a bitch, and from what I heard it must be true.

The Monster can't keep a woman or a job and has contracted hepatitis C.

You can't mess with God's children.

My life will forever be affected by my past.

I still get angry really easily but God is not done with me yet.

I'm a work in progress, I'll tell you that much.

I shut down when I don't want to explain my feelings and bottle them up.

Looking back I ask, WHY?

Why me?

Why didn't I tell anyone?

Why couldn't someone save me?

What was it about me that made me a victim?

I don't know the answers to any of these questions.

I Haven't Told Anyone My Story, But You- Keisha

There's an answer
If you reach into your soul
And the sorrow that you know
Will melt away ~ Mariah Carey

You may know me now, but there's no way you could know me then.

I'm the one that's always smiling and happy to help.

I stay wearing the latest trends.

My face stays beat bi-weekly nail and toe appointments keeps everything on fleek.

Clothes always have designer labels.

Cars paid for.

And as far as my children, there is no difference.

I make my own money, pay my own bills.

I'm good.

I won't walk out the front door without looking like I walked out of a magazine spread.

These messy bitches will never get the chance to say I ain't fly.

They don't have anything on me.

These hoes ain't, wait let me stop.

I don't talk like that; hold on I got too comfortable with you.

None of these females are even in my league.

I don't worry about keeping up with the Joneses.

Hell, I am the Joneses.

I have Lupus.

I live a lie.

I'm not as happy as I may seem.

If I look in the mirror too long I see that scared, thrown away little girl I've been running from.

She's weak and flawed.

She's been used, abused, and talked about.

She's dead.

My hair comes out and my skin is covered in rashes.

I was tormented for so many years that I became numb to the hate.

I was called ugly so much that I started to believe it.

My hair was sometimes really kinky because the relaxer would burn my scalp so bad that I couldn't stand for them to stay on long enough to straighten my hair.

That is why I never miss a hair appointment now.

I've been going to the same hairdresser since I was in the tenth grade.

When my scalp is bad, she knows how to treat it or just shampoo it and find a protective style.

I've always been good at keeping up this façade, but I'm so tired.

I'm falling apart on the inside, and although I smile and always have my head up.

I don't have anyone I can trust to help me get through this.

I won't allow myself to break down in front of my children;

I bought my second house, and I was moving up in the law firm.

That, alone, is amazing because I had my daughter while I was a senior in high school.

Everybody told me I'd be lucky to land a city job with benefits, but anything would be a step in the right direction.

It all started with my daughter's father, Bear, my first love.

I fell hard and fast.

He was older and more experienced than I.

Bear said all the right things and talked me into his bed.

Our relationship lasted until our daughter was five.

He just couldn't leave the streets alone.

He paid for me to go to school, and not work for a few years while raising our daughter.

He understood that I was trying to better myself.

I graduated from college twice, and he was still trying to be a street pharmacist.

When I left, he gave me everything I needed to continue chasing my career.

When our daughter turned nine, he was murdered after a chick set him up to be robbed.

I was so devastated.

When I met my son's father, Nick, I just wanted a warm body, and he knew it.

He used me and treated me so bad.

He drove around in my nice car, which was paid for by my daughter's father, all day.

While I was at work, he played video games and cheated with all kinds of tramps.

He cheated on me and broke me down mentally to the point I stopped eating.

I didn't keep myself up.

I fell right into his web.

He made me believe that no one would want me.

He pawned my car title without my knowledge, and my car was taken away.

He said I was hanging out too much, so he made me cut off all my friends and family.

He was all I had left.

I worked full time while he stayed home with our son.

He wanted to be a rapper, and I was footing the bill for his rapper career that was "going to take off any day now".

I paid for mixtapes and studio time.

I allowed my daughter's grandmother to raise her.

I did not want her to witness my self-destruction.

She wanted something of her son's to hold on to, so it worked out for the both of us.

I was so thankful to her for that.

By the time I was able to care for my daughter again she wouldn't know me.

Hell, I didn't know me I was a different person.

I was broken.

I know God doesn't make any mistakes.

We were supposed to be practicing safe sex when I got pregnant with my son.

Although my son has been my saving grace, I didn't need to bring him into the world like that.

I had one child that wasn't with me, and I didn't want to lose another.

I came home from work early because my son wasn't feeling well that morning only to find another chick was laid up in my house.

Nick had the nerve to defend her.

He told me I was disrespectful, and she was nice enough to sell us some of her food stamps.

He was just repaying her in my house, in my bed.

It wasn't until then that I reached rock bottom.

I finally got away from him, but at a huge cost.

He beat me so bad, messed up my face and hair.

He told me, "If people knew what you really looked like under all that expensive ass makeup and hair, they would hate yo ass."

He said I wasn't pretty and he never loved me.

That he just got with me to spend up my money, and the sex has been horrible since our first time.

I ran to my parent's house to get my stepfather's gun because there was no way I would allow him to keep hurting me.

I had enough.

That wasn't the first time he said ugly things and smacked me around, but somehow I knew it would be the last

I knew my children would be burying me if I didn't walk away.

When I returned, my neighbor said she had called the police, and he fled, I had my stepfather and stepbrother move my stuff out.

I was so ashamed looking at my face in the mirror, the pain showed through.

I knew I couldn't go anywhere looking the way I did, so I lost my job.

I couldn't face the world.

I stayed in my mother's guest room for seven months feeling sorry for myself.

I blamed myself for everything that went wrong.

I really had to do some soul searching. I went to therapy.

I got a better job and got my shit together.

Although, it took eight years, I met a new man, Jamal.

He is younger than I am and doesn't have as many goals as I do.

I know he'll learn to love me because I am more mature now.

He will grow up later.

My children love him, and he loves them.

He has four kids, and we're a big blended "Brady Bunch" family, except for his ghetto ass baby mamas.

Yep, it's three of them.

I knew going into this that I was the breadwinner.

I went into this with my eyes wide open hoping for the best but preparing for the worst.

I had been knocked down but came up swinging, so I knew I could take on this type of relationship.

Plus, Jamal has never hit me, only pushed to get me out of his face.

I put him out for a few days.

His makeup sex made me forget what we fought about.

Even though he can't keep a job longer than a month or two he still tries.

He picks up the kids when I can't.

He fixes things around the house.

Most importantly he puts it down in the bedroom.

I definitely have no complaints there.

I get to have this chocolate brother on my arm and watch other females turn green with envy when we're out.

Yes, he flirts some, but I know he doesn't want to be with any of them.

Even with all those thirsty broads that stay in his inbox on Facebook and text his phone.

They are no competition for what I give; I'm stability.

No, I do not have the best body or the greatest looks.

He doesn't complain when I'm sick.

He holds down the household and nurses me back to good health.

I'm hoping this is my last relationship.

I'm ready to be married because I've had enough bad apples.

My only issue is he has a passcode on his phone that I can't get into.

I trust him, otherwise.

Why would he leave me?

I'm a total package I cook, and I clean.

I give head that's out of this world, and I pay my own way.

I do the wining and dining, and I'm okay with that because the trade off is mind blowing.

I allow him time to do his thing, play video games, go out without me, and I put a little bit of money in his pockets.

Trust me, I know he's just young and has some growing up to do.

I can hold out.

There is no reason on God's green Earth; I would mature this man up for the next female to enjoy.

He's mine.

I am not doing all this for nothing.

I know I keep repeating the immaturity, I guess I'm just trying to convince myself.

Maybe if I pay for him to enroll in some type of trade school to guarantee employment.

It can help us grow closer, and make him more responsible.

Bringing in some money couldn't hurt anything because I can't keep paying his child support and all of our bills.

Lately, he and my daughter don't get along, but I think it's only because she misses her father.

I'm sure if there is more she'd tell me about it; we're close enough.

If there were something wrong with their relationship, I'd drop his ass like a bad habit.

I've had a couple nice guys hit on me at regular places like the gas station, the car wash, the kids' school, and those men are definitely my type.

I need a man with a warm body and working rod, but I won't stand for a man who mistreats my kids.

I've seen too many weak women chose men over their children, but I am not one of those women.

I can do bad all by myself.

I refuse to have another man ruin my life, and then I have to start over from rock bottom again.

I'm stronger than I have ever been.

I'm at a different point in my life.

Not So "Super" Woman- Ashley

*Even when I'm a mess I still put on a vest with
an S on my chest Oh yes
I'm a Superwoman ~Alicia Keys*

I'm a single mother.

I'm all my kids have.

If I don't work, we don't eat.

I was tired and hurting, but I still had work to do.

As mothers, we always do what we have to do, not what we want to do.

So many nights I've had to cry myself to sleep because I couldn't handle it.

Some kind of way my God always showed up and showed out!

Now what I can't understand is, according to them folks at the Human Service office, I make too much to qualify for food stamps and Medicaid.

I hate them bitches.

They act like giving me a hundred dollars in food stamps gone come out of their checks.

They so freaking stingy with that shit.

My application was denied because I made forty-three dollars over the limit.

I started out as a CNA, but after being there for eight years and developing a relationship with a physician, I was offered tuition assistance, and I became an RN.

I worked that doctor's office during the day and overtime at night in the ER.

I have to work every piece of overtime that's offered at the hospital.

I sometimes worked 16-hour days around the holidays.

Even when I was tired, I never allowed my boys to see me hurt or sad.

I never want them to think they could possibly be the reason I hurt because my kids are my greatest gifts.

There were times I had to ride the bus with two kids screaming and hollering, and everyone on the bus used to look at me funny.

I got tired of that and saved up to buy myself a car.

I never ask for help from their sorry ass daddy, Dexter.

Sometimes, the deadbeat pays his child support, and sometimes he doesn't.

I don't let that stop me from doing my best.

I'm raising men.

I can't be soft around them or with them.

I knew I shouldn't have ignored the pain I was feeling, but I couldn't take off to go to the doctor.

I hadn't met my deductible.

I couldn't afford to take off and lose money for the doctor to tell me that he couldn't find anything wrong, but take these pills and go see this specialist.

That specialist would just run more tests and cost me more money that I didn't have to waste.

I did what I could.

I dealt with the pain on my own at first, but it got worse after about six months, and I begin taking over the counter pain meds.

The scary part was when I woke up in the back of an ambulance; apparently, I passed out at my day job at the physicians' office.

They had no choice but to call an ambulance to have me transported to the hospital.

I told them I was okay.

I was weak because I skipped breakfast and wasn't really sleeping well and maybe a little dehydrated.

The hospital kept me for three days running tests, and that's when they told me I had stage 2 breast cancer.

I was devastated.

I had no idea I was that sick.

The first thing I asked was: what I would tell my boys?

I was all they had, literally.

How is it possible that I worked in the hospital and didn't know that anything was wrong with me?

How did I not recognize the signs?

I got my yearly checkup on a regular basis.

I made sure to listen to my body and rest when I could.

All I could think about was my boys being raised by someone that wasn't me.

I couldn't do that to them.

If their daddy did at least half of what the law required, then maybe I wouldn't have to work myself close to death, without a backup plan.

How did I manage to pick the sorriest man in America to procreate with?

Dexter was perfect man that did all the right things before the first baby was born.

After our second son, he decided that he wasn't into women anymore.

Did I turn him gay?

Was having sex with me that bad?

As far as I knew, we were fine and everything was going well.

I knew he had been spending a lot of time with Gerald because our sons were on the same baseball team together.

Hell, I didn't think they were sleeping together.

Gerald's wife, Christine, caught them in her bed together and sent me videos, pictures, texts, and more than I cared to see.

I was literally sick to my stomach seeing that crap.

Two grown married men carrying on a **secret** relationship was the worst.

There is no way on earth I can leave my boys behind to be raised by them.

Gerald's wife and I became friends after we got over our initial disgust for them.

We were trying to figure what was wrong with our vaginas to turn to straight men gay.

Once their **secret** was out, they made it clear that they would be in a relationship together.

They both left us and got their own place together.

I find it very funny that they are living the life I had seen for myself, my happily ever after.

Christine was the first person I told about the cancer.

She was the one that sat up at the hospital while I was in surgery.

She took care of the boys when I was too sick to care for them, along with her three kids.

My kids stayed over at her house more then they stayed at home.

Even though the kids didn't know it they were practically siblings, Gerald and Christine had two girls and a boy.

They are good kids.

By the grace of God, the cancer is in remission.

I'm working again.

I don't work as hard as I use to.

I demanded that Dexter pays child support and step up in raising our boys.

The only rule: he and Gerald can't act as a couple in the presence of the five children.

We have finally gotten to a point where we can co-parent and I'm okay with that.

With my cancer diagnosis, I learned that I am not superwoman.

I cannot do it all by myself.

It's okay to ask for help every now and then.

I may even start dating again, once my hair and nails grow back.

Why Wasn't I Enough? - Val

My faith kept me alive I picked myself back up,
I hold my head up high I was not built to break
I didn't know my own strength ~Whitney
Houston

On the outside, I appear to be a whole package, the picture of perfection.

I'm pharmaceutical sales rep, and I make good money.

I've been doing this for sixteen years now.

Although, it's not what I wanted for my career, at least it pays the bills.

Plus, I'm the only local rep, and I have made numerous connections.

I wanted to be an accountant with my own firm, but I got married to Lance.

I was submissive and stupid, but I felt trapped and needed out.

I wear a mask every day pretending to be happy and whole.

It's a lie.

If I were really honest with myself, I'd admit that I knew my marriage wouldn't last.

We were only together for 13 months when he asked me to marry him.

Four days later we were standing in front of the Justice of the peace, saying, "I do."

It wasn't the wedding I dreamt of and he wasn't my dream husband.

I was blinded by love and would've followed him to the ends of the earth.

If he told me the sky was pink, I'd go right along with that.

We were always into some freaky stuff: threesomes, dominatrix, swinging, and strip clubs.

The moment I found out I was pregnant, I no longer had any interests in doing anything that could cause any harm to my baby.

I had matured up and no longer felt the need to participate in the wild risky sexual behavior.

He wanted to do it anyways with or without me.

I begged him to stop, but he showed me that his desire was to live life like a bachelor.

I couldn't compete with his desires to sleep around.

He chose that lifestyle over the kids and me.

I was in an involuntary open marriage.

I'm completely broken inside.

If it weren't for my father and my kids I would've ended it all years ago, but I can't leave them.

I'm literally all they have, and they're all I have honestly.

My mother passed when I was eleven from injuries she sustained in a car crash.

There was whispering that she suffered from depression caused by my daddy's numerous affairs.

She was speeding and drove her car directly into a tree ending her life.

I was young didn't know much about the things that were going on in our house.

I know my mother always seemed sad and she cried a lot.

I was a young girl that needed my mommy, and she was gone.

My daddy had plenty of lady friends, but they weren't my mama.

I wasn't interested in any of them trying to take her place.

My sister and I are 7 years apart, so she was away at college when mommy died.

She knew nothing about daddy's affairs or of mommy's depression.

She had gotten into some trouble on campus and was put out of school.

She became addicted to drugs and then a lesbian.

She cut us off after she stole my whole medicine bag, and I had to file a police report on her.

She got arrested, with her dumb ass.

She only stole cholesterol pills and a new psoriasis drug that has no street value at all.

There was no way I was about to go down for any mess like that.

Yes, I turned her in.

My daddy got sick about eight years ago.

He has cirrhosis of the liver from years and years of drinking after the death of my mom.

He blames himself for driving her crazy.

For years, I blamed him too.

Now I feel responsible for him and making sure he's comfortable for the time he has left.

No matter what may have happened, he's my father and I love him so being there for him was not a question.

I had to put my father into an assisted living home.

The guilt of it caused me to have panic attacks.

My now ex-husband would not do his part around the house while I was making the money.

He stayed home all day because he was getting a little disability check.

He worked at a local manufacturing plant and supposedly hurt his back.

Anyway, that was before we were married.

He refused to help me with my father's care because my father never liked him.

I couldn't allow my father to be mistreated.

I was so stressed out about not being there for my dad and putting an end to my failing marriage.

Lance had the audacity to think I couldn't make it without him.

I don't really go out at all, except for an occasional drink with the girls after work.

I'm always getting invites to parties, fundraisers, and banquets; I always decline.

I would feel guilty if I wasn't there for my father and my kids.

It's a group of about seven us that work in this area.

I wouldn't really call them friends because I don't tell them my personal business.

They just think I have a busy social life when I turn down their invites.

Sometimes, I just like to be alone.

With so much on my shoulders, I need to be able to close my door and remove the "S" from my chest.

I couldn't take it any longer after arguing with him one night and I jumped in my car and just drove until I almost ran out of gas.

I checked into the closest hotel around, and cried all night.

I also took one too many Valiums sometime during the early morning.

I thought I knew how many I could take that would end it all.

It wasn't until housekeeping came to clean the room that I realized I was still alive, and my heart still hurt.

I can't even remember what they looked like, but they helped me into a cold shower.

I begged the two small Hispanic women not to call 911, and in return, I gave them $200 each for their discretion.

I sometimes wonder if they were to see me out somewhere would they remember me, and expose my **secret** from that night.

I went home like nothing ever happened.

I lay in bed for seven days.

I felt as though I had no reason to get up and go on.

How could I let this happen?

How could I let him make me so weak?

My body was tired and my heart was torn.

He had taken me to hell and back.

He belittled me, called me crazy, and tried to take my kids.

He said would expose all the nasty things we did together including leaking our homemade sex tapes with other couples.

I never thought that those things would come back and haunt me this way.

He told me I was his biggest regret, even tried to get alimony from me.

The balls of this unemployed lowlife jerk wanting money from me.

I almost considered my cousin's offer to break his legs, but I knew that would somehow end up costing me money.

I told him that was not necessary.

Yet.

I know it sounds bad but I'd love to see him get his ass kicked for all he has put me through.

The thought alone of hearing his bones break makes me smile on the inside.

It took time for me to bounce back after that, but I did, and I thought I was stronger than ever until I met Delante on Facebook.

He was my rebound boy toy, but he was out of my league.

I knew it.

I was having fun until I got tired of playing house and wanted more, and just like that.

He left.

I was back in a slump but this time I turned to alcohol to numb me.

I didn't want to feel anything.

I take Valium with Hennessey when the voices in my head become too chaotic.

But when I'm at my lowest my mother appears to guide me.

She always helps me pull myself back up.

I'm not crazy or anything 'cause I ain't like those people on the streets walking around talking to themselves.

I am raising healthy happy kids, looking in on my father, and going to work.

I could control my drinking.

Besides, I only drank for peace of mind.

I wonder if the same voices pushed my mother over the edge and forced her to escape her own mind, ending her life.

That's the one question my mama will not answer when she comes to me.

Why?

Why did you leave us?

She gets upset.

I won't see her for days.

I always apologize and beg her to come back.

She does when I need her the most.

Sure my mama had a few drinks the day she died.

But she should've been remembered for all the great things she had done.

She owned her own business, organized charity events, started a battered women's foundation, and spent her free time volunteering at the Children's Hospital.

However, all people dwell on that she had been drinking.

I didn't understand all the weight she carried whiling appearing so strong on the outside.

I don't want to ever reach that breaking point.

I can't ask for help.

I don't want to appear weak.

I was drinking in between clients during the day.

On weekends I drank all day.

I only left out my house to buy alcohol.

The cashiers at the stores near my house knew me.

I started driving further out each time.

I was too tired to do my normal routines.

My ex-husband filed for custody.

I know he didn't want the kids.

He just didn't want to pay child support.

He just did it to hurt me.

I stopped going to the beauty salon and started buying wigs.

I heard they were all talking about me behind my back.

My stylist had the nerve to ask if I had a drinking problem.

Like it was any of her damn business.

I've heard them gossiping about some of the other clients at the salon, and I knew they would talk about me too.

I couldn't trust them anymore.

They weren't the only ones I couldn't trust.

Everybody in my family was whispering about what they thought they knew about me.

I heard my aunt say that we all got a little bit of the crazies just like my grandmother.

I heard that my grandmother had been locked away for running down her sister's live-in boyfriend.

I didn't think she was crazy at all for doing something her sister should have done in the beginning.

I didn't care about what anybody said until my kids asked me about not wanting them anymore.

I don't know why they asked me that kind of question.

They are the reason I'm still able to have an ounce of hope for myself.

How did I get to this point?

I'm at rock bottom.

How did I neglect the people that I love and care about the most?

I had to take some time off of work for a while, but that was about up.

I just need an outlet 'cause I feel like I'm losing my mind.

I have to get it together before I self-destruct and lose my house and kids.

Hell, maybe I'll start dating women, try something different altogether.

I allowed my love for the wrong man to break me down to someone I didn't even know.

Now I'm paying for it.

Loose Hips- Leslie

I keep letting you back in
How can I explain myself?
As painful as this thing has been
I just can't be with no one else ~Lauryn Hill

I'm a big boned girl.

I've always been bigger than other girls around me.

It doesn't faze me one bit.

I'm used to it by now.

It's not like I eat a lot.

I'm just big, not really what you would call fat.

I ain't never missed a meal either.

I know what my limits are.

I've tried to lose weight, but nothing seems to work.

I did the soup diet, the cabbage, and the shakes, Weight Watchers, Jenny Craig.

I've had more gym memberships than I care to remember.

I can live with being big although it comes with its' problems.

I've always been called "big black girl"

I've spent my whole life trying not to be bitter about the cards life has dealt me.

I cry sometimes thinking back on the ugly names I've been called.

My feelings used to be so hurt hearing all the cruel things said about me, over something I couldn't control.

I didn't choose to be big.

I just am.

I have a few close friends but I don't think they're all that genuine.

I feel like they keep me around so that I make them look better.

When we go out, all the guys are only looking at them.

Sometimes, they get them to buy me a drink out of like sympathy or whatever.

I never accept those.

I don't want their pity.

Plus, I'm not checking for them.

I have someone that puts a little money in my pockets, buys me nice gifts, wash my car, take out the trash, and mow the lawn.

My man massages my feet without me asking, he sends flowers and candy.

He treats me like a queen.

But I share him with his wife.

I think she may have an idea that he has someone on the side.

But I'm more than just a "side chick".

He has introduced us before.

She thinks I'm his cousin that just moved here from out of town.

He loves me just the way I am.

Whenever I talk about losing weight, he gets mad.

He wants me to stay the way I am.

He said he couldn't do anything with a small chick.

He loves all my curves and especially my big butt.

He's only staying with her for the benefits of her taking care of him and their children.

They have two kids together and he has two other outside kids, and she takes care of them plus her older daughter.

He always tells me that we'll be together soon.

Until then I just wait on him to call or text when she's not around or even sometimes when she is around.

Those conversations are usually short like "Hi, whatcha you doing?

Okay, I'll hit you up later" and I know he tells her I was one of his homeboys.

He keeps a key to my house and car so he can let himself in and out whenever he wants to.

I've tried to picture myself with someone else and it doesn't work.

He controls the strings to my heart and he pulls them according to his needs.

I hate the fact that I have to hide our relationship.

He says he has too much to lose if anybody knew about me, so I play my part.

I've tried to date other guys but he gets so jealous that I feel bad and I break it off with them.

Those are the times I see how much I mean to him.

I want the kids and the white picket fence fairytale with him.

I've been pregnant twice.

The first time he begged me to get an abortion.

He said his daughter was just too young for him to leave his family, and he needed to be home.

He doesn't want his kids growing up without their father the way he did.

I understood, so I had my cousin take me to the clinic while he was at home being Mr. Husband.

The second time, I miscarried at home alone when he had taken his family on vacation.

I sent him texts asking him to please come get me, but he never replied.

I checked his Facebook page.

There he was sharing pictures of him and that bitch in Gatlinburg.

I was so pissed that he was showing her off to the world while keeping me his little **secret**.

I sent him a picture of the bloodstained sheets that would have exposed our **secret** relationship along with a text that read:

It's over. I saw you on FB with her. I lost our baby while you were playing house. I'm changing my *locks and my number. I can't continue to allow you to hurt me while she's winning. I'm blocking you on FB. If you ever really cared for me, please leave me alone. Leave me alone to find a man that will love me for me, and not just in **secret**. I can't be your side chick no more. Leslie*

I want to leave.

I don't think anyone else would love me as much as he does.

It isn't like there's a line of men waiting to get with me.

I'm not that small sexy type.

Of course, as soon as he could, he sent me an I'm sorry text begging me to forgive him

I'm not stupid.

I did get my number and locks changed.

I was ignoring him.

He kept sending me flowers and gifts.

I was done and ready to move on with my life.

He knows how weak I am for him.

I don't know why I need him.

I just can't be without a man.

He's a good man,

He's just in a bad situation.

Half of a man is better than no man at all, right?

Just like that, I'm back at his beck and call.

After he showed up at my job crying, saying he couldn't live without me, and he filed for divorce.

He said he was ready to be with me and only me.

That was two years ago.

He still belongs to his wife, but at least she knows about me now.

She followed him to my house one night and saw that he let himself in with his key.

Our relationship was exposed.

She attempted suicide by sitting with her car running in their garage.

I guess it's true that God does look out for babies and fools.

The idiot wrote a goodbye letter to him and everything.

He called me all upset and angry.

He explained to me that he needed to stay with her just long enough for her to get better.

I cried into the phone, but not for her, for myself, because I knew what that meant.

He wasn't leaving her.

He assured me that it was so she couldn't hurt herself or their kids.

He said that he wouldn't be able to live with himself if she killed herself because of him.

He did tell me he doesn't have sex with her.

He resents her for keeping us apart.

I know that he loves me and only me.

He stays over at my house at least 3 nights a week.

If he didn't love me why he would introduce me to his kids and their cool with it, I guess.

His mama is another issue.

I don't think she likes me.

She doesn't have to 'cause I ain't sleeping with her.

I wish I didn't need him.

He's probably the best I can get.

Sometimes, I wish his wife had killed herself.

I know it's wrong but that's how my heart feels.

Don't go judging me.

'Cause you don't understand my self-esteem is not the greatest.

He makes me feel like I'm enough.

We have been together too long, but I can't wait for him.

I don't plan to wait forever.

I'm gone at least see where this leads us.

'Cause he said we can start trying for another baby soon.

My Mother's Daughter- Toni

Dear mama, place no one above ya, sweet lady You are appreciated, don't cha know we love ya? ~Tupac

Oh, so you heard huh?

It's not a **secret** anymore.

My husband cheats, and I prayed for him to stop.

I can't make him, okay?

I love him and the Bible says I need to stay in my marriage.

I've heard the whispers behind my back when you think I'm not listening at the kids' school.

I see the "she's so stupid" stares and snickers on my job.

I catch the side eyes at church.

I talked to the Pastor and he assured me I was doing the right thing.

My husband said he was done with the cheating.

He just needed to get it out of his system.

He said he was young, dumb and full of you know what when we first got married.

He thought he was ready for our family life.

He got caught up out there with his single friends.

They were living in bachelor pads, with lots of fast women and even faster cars, and single life seems so far away.

He thought he was missing something and needed to get back to it.

One night, he was at one of his Frat brother's house and some strippers came through.

He slept with one.

It was his first time cheating.

When he came home, he didn't have the heart to tell me what happened.

So he lied to keep from hurting me because he loves me.

After that, I felt a shift in my marriage.

Some of that woman's intuitions my Big Mama told me about.

But I ignored it.

I knew he was up to something because we didn't have sex daily like we used to.

He always said he was too tired.

Over the next two years, he had three regular women that he slept with.

I heard the humming coming from his pocket while we were alone, and then he all of a sudden had to leave.

I watched him take the phone that I paid the bill on, in the bathroom with him every time he went.

I bought everything right down to the gas for the car so I guess I paid for his affairs also.

I found receipts for condoms, hotels, and dinners, but they must've been paying.

He didn't have any money, unless I gave it to him.

At least he buying condoms now, especially after the time he gave me Herpes.

Then one day, one of his side pieces called my phone talking out the side of her neck saying,

"He doesn't love you anymore.

He wants a divorce and he knows you gone beg him to stay because you're just that pathetic.

He doesn't feel like going through that, so he stays, but he really wants to be with me."

That time I stayed away for about seven months.

I was crushed like my world had just been rocked, but I needed him.

I needed my marriage, what would people say?

I need a man.

I can't be alone.

I don't know how to be.

I've always had a man, any man, no matter how he treated me.

I prayed to God to send me this man.

When He did I promised Him that I'd stay married, no matter the price.

My husband has slapped me twice, but he had been drinking and I pushed him first.

I have loved him since I first met him.

I was in a bad first marriage and my husband rescued me.

He filled a void that had been missing my whole life.

The hole made my daddy created when left my mama and me for a younger, prettier, thinner high yellow heffa.

Momma, well, she was dealing with her own insecurities.

She was busy doing her own thing with different so-called "uncles" and male friends, who walked in and out of our lives like a revolving door.

She was my role model.

I learned from the best, depending on how you look at it.

Plus, I do have some insecurities of my own about my looks.

I ain't no size two.

I've always been called black and ugly.

I hate anything dark.

As a kid, I used household bleach on my skin.

It burned and only caused sores and ugly scabs that I picked at.

I'm not proud to be black.

That is why my husband is white.

Oh did I forget to mention that?

I wasn't even proud of our first black President Obama.

Hell, he was mixed too.

I didn't want my kids to suffer like I did being black and ugly.

But of course, they face different kinds of race-related issues from both sides of our families.

They've been called everything from Oreos, zebras, and pandas to half-breeds and mutts.

Even in 2017, people act as if being biracial is such a bad thing.

It is still not as bad as being dark with nappy hair.

If I lose husband number two, then that's something else I failed at.

So to keep him I let him be and don't bother him.

Eventually, he'll get bored with those side chicks, come back home, and apologize with gifts of flowers, cards, and chocolates.

I always forgive him.

It's called love.

You know "till death do us part".

I can't keep female friends because I never know when he'll want to screw them.

So I do things to push them away; then, when times get hard, and they always do.

I don't have anyone to turn to.

I always end up going to my Pastor for a counseling.

Maybe I'll take up a Pilates or Yoga class.

I've even tried hang with some his Republican friends' wives, but even they sometimes treat me as a 'step and fetch it'.

I've already taken so many prescriptions that I'm numb to feeling anything.

I might need some illegal drugs.

My meddling mama calls him a dog without a leash screwing everything around.

It's not like my mama is in a position to judge.

However, that's just her personality, you know, the judgmental hypocrite.

She is always offering unsolicited advice because nothing I ever did was right in her eyes.

At least I am trying to live according to the Bible with my husband.

I love my mom, but she can't give me what my husband can.

Nobody can.

I stay and I pray that it's a phase he's going through.

Judge me if you must.

Trust me I've heard it all before.

Until you have walked in my shoes you don't really know what it takes to be me.

Quite frankly, you can't speak on the decisions I make as a grown ass woman.

Save your opinions on my life.

I didn't need any then and I don't need any now.

I'm doing me and doing just fine.

Thank you!!

Undeniable- Laila

I wonder why we take from our women
Why we rape our women, do we hate our
women?
I think it's time to kill for our women
Time to heal our women, be real to our women
~ Tupac Shakur

Everyone said I would be a high school dropout with a baby on my hip.

But little did they know I was a virgin and proud of it.

I always hung with the guys, so everyone assumed I was having sex.

Then I was raped and became pregnant during my second year of college.

I was afraid and ashamed to tell anyone.

He told me I asked for it.

He blamed me for his actions because we were from the same hometown.

I believed him.

I made his lies my truths.

I should've known something was going to happen.

I just had that bad feeling in my stomach after I agreed to hang out with him.

I've known him for a while now.

I thought we were cool.

I thought we had established a type of closeness where we could be ourselves around the other.

At first, he acted naturally until he offered me something to drink.

I didn't accept it.

Something told me not to drink it.

We sat down to watch a movie and chill, but then he tried to kiss me.

I pushed him off of me and tried to leave.

He grabbed me by the hair and pulled me back down on the couch placing his hand over my mouth

He said, "I like to have rough sex so you fighting me will only make it more enjoyable, but I am going to get it either way."

"Screaming won't help you, it will only turn me on, so just try to enjoy it.

I knew from the first time I met you that I wanted you.

During the campus' orientation last year, I decided I would have you," he stated boldly.

He continued, "The soda I offered you with the "X" in it would have helped you relax but you just wouldn't go for it.

I kinda of figured you wouldn't."

I asked him not to do it, begged him even, to just please let me go.

I wouldn't say anything to anyone.

"What kind of girl wears hoe clothes to class?

Girls like you are always asking for it, then pretending to say no.

You came to my room at night?

What did you think would happen among friends, right?

Who's gonna believe you," he asked me.

He pulled my pants down and ripped my underwear off with one hand, still covering my mouth with the other.

And yes I thought about biting him but it wouldn't give me enough time to get anywhere.

I felt my soul leaving my body with every forceful thrust.

I was hurting so bad I passed out, but not before I saw his devilish smirk of enjoyment.

I prayed to God that he would get tired and stop, but he continued for 674 seconds.

674 seconds of hell I endured while this beast forced his penis into my tight vagina.

The walk back to my room was more torture.

My middle was split and every step felt worse than the one before it.

I was swollen and throbbing but determined to get across campus.

A few students were out that night, but their faces were all a blur to me while I walked what seemed to be the longest green mile.

Once I finally made it back to my room, I showered and lay in bed for the next two days.

I finally got up threw those clothes in the trash, showered again, and went to class.

I wore sweat pants until college graduation.

The guy that raped me was white.

I wasn't his only victim.

The college being in the Bible belt and his parents donating money to the university, they just swept it under the rug.

He was never charged.

He was expelled from the school though but not because of raping me.

I was in denial about my pregnancy until after the second trimester.

I did everything I could to lose that baby, but my son was born just fine.

Once I laid eyes on him, I knew I'd love him forever.

It was summer break when Jaden was born.

Jaden was on the small side due to lack of prenatal care, and his complexion was nothing like anyone in our family.

On top of his complexion, his eyes were the prettiest shade of light blue.

Nobody in my family had blue eyes.

I was on scholarship, so I had to get back and finish getting my degree in education.

I left Jaden with my mother.

Initially, I wanted an education degree, but after I was raped, I decided to pursue a degree in social work in hopes of helping my younger self.

After I graduated, I went back home and started raising my son.

I exposed my **secret** to my mother.

She said she never bought the lie I told her about not knowing who Jaden's father was.

I finally told my mom the truth behind my son's conception, and we cried together.

I was so relieved that she believed me and consoled me.

It was like a heavy burden was lifted off my shoulders when she expressed that she knew already.

She was so sincere with her compassion.

I was stunned but relieved from the weight I carried.

I was doing well up until that day Jaden's sperm donor walked into my office without notice or forewarning.

A feather could've knocked me over as soon as he spoke.

I instantly froze.

Seeing his face immediately took me back to the night he raped me.

Seeing the blood drained from his pale face he remembered that dreadful night as well.

He was sad that his sister recently passed away.

He was trying to get assistance with getting custody of her children; all I heard was blah, blah, blah.

All of a sudden, I had a flashback of him saying, "I wanted you and then during the campus orientations last year I decided I would have you.

The soda I offered you with the "X" it in would help you relax but you just wouldn't go for it."

Life can be a bitch sometimes, just so happen that Jaden's first word was "Dada" and now at six he was starting to ask questions about where his "dad' was?

I was working and raising my son.

Why would God allow this devil to waltz into my office and ask me for help?

Those kids would be better off with Casey Anthony as a guardian than this serial rapist.

I closed my eyes briefly and shook my head to rid my thoughts that were invaded by the demons of my past.

I excused myself and darted from my office to gather my thoughts.

I went to my supervisor's office and explained to her the situation, and she completely understood.

She followed me back down the hall.

I knew we'd caught him off guard when he dropped that devilish grin off his face.

I caught a glimpse of what he was smiling at; it was a picture of Jaden and me, it was misplaced on my desk.

He knows, was all that I was thinking.

I was noticeably shaken up.

My supervisor informed him that we could not offer him any services.

I couldn't look him in the face as he stood up to leave.

I hid behind my supervisor to avoid his stare.

I held my breath until he walked out of the Crisis Center.

I was never prepared to see him, EVER.

I felt the evil presence in the air.

He had to know that Jaden is his son.

The proof is in my son's eyes.

In My Sister's Shadow- Brooke

'Cause you were my sister, my strength and my pride
only God may know why,
Still, I will get by ~ Brandy

I don't even know how I got with Dee's fat ass.

I've never liked big guys, and I dodged him every way I could trying to be nice.

Eventually, he wore me down.

I said yes to a date with him.

He bought flowers and sent chocolates to my job.

He would even buy gifts for my daughter and son.

I really admired because I had never let him meet them.

I wasn't the type of girl that will let every man she dates to meet her kids.

I ain't that stupid.

I met Derek aka Dee in the mall, where I worked as a makeup artist.

I was getting lunch at the food court not paying attention.

I spilled my soda on his jacket that was sitting on the chair next to my table.

I was so embarrassed.

He was so nice about it.

He and I had been friends for about four years.

He had been asking me out to a movie for the 100th time.

I finally agreed.

He was such a gentleman.

He made me feel comfortable, secure, and he had money.

He was the answer I had been searching for.

I needed him because he gave the confidence I never had.

To be honest Dee helped me with my own insecurities.

Secretly, I envied my older sister, Katrina to the point I hated her sometimes.

She was book smart with street creditability, beautiful inside, and outside.

Katrina always seems to have it together.

She is what you would call all that.

Katrina could never do wrong in my parents' eyes.

They worshiped the ground she walked on.

"Katrina's so smart.

Katrina's room is always cleaned.

Katrina never gives us any trouble.

Katrina's beautiful.

Katrina is great at everything she does," was all I used to hear them say.

It was like she was the golden child.

I was a failure and the black sheep of the family.

I never believed that crap about parents not having a favorite kid.

I lived it firsthand.

I always feel like I'm in competition with her.

Everyone always asks, "Where's the pretty one?"

I cried so many nights asking God, "to take me away from here."

I always felt I was born only to make Katrina look better, so they would know what to measure her to.

I always felt like a complete failure.

Katrina went to college to become this successful attorney who would take care of our parents and save the world.

Here I am a single mother with two kids and no husband working at the mall.

I settled for Derek because he took me, damaged goods with baggage.

There is no love in our relationship.

Well, I guess he loves me.

But the feeling isn't mutual.

I mean, I guess I will eventually learn to love him.

He's a great father to my children and an excellent provider.

There's no romance on my part.

I just have sex with him because that's what comes along with the territory, but for me, it's more like a show, that I auditioned for.

Katrina envied me for a hot second when Derek asked me to marry him at our parents' house on Christmas with a *phat* ring and a brand new car.

That's probably the only reason I said yes.

I even managed to squeeze a few tears out.

The look of green painted across Katrina's face was priceless.

She made up some story about having to leave.

Seeing that made saying yes worth it.

But the cherry on top was calling her the next day asking her to be my bridesmaid.

Even over the phone, I heard the jealousy in her voice.

Katrina said "of course," then made up something and ended our conversation.

Katrina couldn't keep a good man.

Lil Miss Perfect can't keep a man.

So far couldn't have kids but spoiled my two like crazy.

Even they loved "Aunty Trin" more than they loved me.

I dragged her and momma to multiple dress stores, cake tastings and potential venues for my wedding.

I noticed that Katrina did all of them with a smile plastered on her face and I thought, "she's a damn good actress."

The week before my wedding, my momma pulled me to the side.

She told me "I know that you are finding joy out of taunting your big sister with this wedding.

I'm telling you right now to ease off.

She doesn't deserve that.

She's been nice and did every little crazy wedding thing you've asked of her.

It ends now, I'm not asking, I'm telling you. It's over."

I knew better than to disrespect her.

I was so angry with my mother that I only allowed my father to walk me down the aisle.

I stopped intentionally trying to get under my sister's skin instantly.

That only freed up more time for me to let the reality of being married to a man that I didn't love sink in.

My honeymoon was the worst night of my life.

He was so excited.

I drank so much at the reception.

I was so sick and couldn't have sex that night.

So it all worked out for me on that part.

Perfect Katrina was there to nurse me back to health.

She told me how happy she was for us and that I was doing the right thing for my children.

I still remember thinking how sincere she sounded and maybe we could finally be friends after all.

I started to change my feelings towards my big sister.

I realized that instead of hating her for who she was that maybe I should try to be more like her.

Katrina and I started from that point being friends.

She confided in me about this new guy she was seeing, Terry.

He started out as a client but her partner ended up taking his case so she could date him.

Terry was tall dark and handsome like our father and a natural charmer.

We all liked him.

Katrina and I started doing sister days every other Saturday, and I noticed that she had a bruise on her arm.

She told me that she bumped into her car door one day getting in.

I believed her.

After about four months into our routine, she started canceling on me.

Making up excuses as to why we couldn't meet, and not allowing me to come see her.

The fourth of July was always at our parent's house, and Katrina was late.

That wasn't like her.

I volunteered to go check on her.

When I pulled up, the hairs on my back stood straight up.

Katrina's house was dark and cold.

I let myself in through the garage.

I saw her car was there with her keys and purse inside.

I called her name, and she didn't answer.

While walking through flipping on lights, I panicked when I saw furniture thrown around.

My heart sank when I didn't get an answer from her but saw bloody handprints on the wall leading upstairs.

I began to run up them two at a time until I reached her bedroom.

There she was on the floor, covered in blood dead with her eyes wide open.

Her phone was on her stomach with my parents' number displayed.

She was trying to call for help.

I grabbed my phone from my pocket and dialed 911.

While waiting for an answer, I fell down next to my sister.

I put her head in my lap and caressed her face.

I was sobbing uncontrollably attempting to tell the operator to send an ambulance and the police.

My sister had been stabbed in the chest and stomach and she had bruises on her face and neck.

On her bedroom floor, I saw a trail of blood with large footprints.

I didn't even think about if Katrina's attacker was still in the house.

I became frightened and called Dee.

I told him what happened and he told me, "Say no more.

I'm on my way."

I guess this is the reason I learned to love him.

He always puts me first whenever I need him.

Within 15 minutes, the police had arrived and everything was taped off.

The police and CSI were swarming the house.

It took three men to pry me away from my sister's body.

When Derek arrived he was stopped before he could get to the driveway.

I screamed at the cop to let him in.

I needed him.

I need him don't I?

It took losing my big sister for me to realize I needed Dee, my knight and shining armor.

The police found Terry's body in the bathroom downstairs with a gunshot wound to the head.

It was ruled a murder-suicide.

We later learned Terry was a habitual woman beater.

Those were some charges he had when Katrina's firm was representing him.

I was so sick.

 She had broken so many of our dates because he wouldn't let her come or she was hiding the bruises from me.

How could I not know?

My parents thought he was a good guy and they trusted dude.

They didn't know either.

Dee asked around but nobody knew Terry or about his horrific past.

I can't sleep or eat because every time I close my eyes I see my big sister's face the night I found her.

She was so naïve.

She saw the good in everyone, no matter how much of a monster we were.

Every day we found out something new that made the situation worse.

Katrina was pregnant but didn't want to have a baby out of wedlock.

I guess she learned from my mistake.

Katrina tried to prevent accidents like an unwanted pregnancy.

She told me she never wanted kids.

Terry began to threaten her to make her keep the baby.

She knew the procedure.

She had an order of protection.

Her firm knew not to allow Terry to come harass her there.

He snapped and killed my sister because he was a sick punk.

A coward.

He took the easy way out by killing himself.

I wanted to be the one that killed him.

My beautiful big sister was forever gone.

I wasted so much of that time being jealous and hating her.

I should've been getting to know her better.

I'll never understand how a man could take the lives of the women they swore to love.

I live with the guilt every day of not saying something when I first noticed the bruises or her change in attitude.

A year later, I had another baby girl who we agreed to name Katrina.

I never questioned how or why I got with Derek again.

When I look into baby Katrina's eyes I see my sister.

I know he is the whole reason I have her.

He saved me because I could've easily found a Terry.

I'm in the process of working with Katrina's firm to get a charity or scholarship program in her name.

I hope to prevent this continued cycle of women being killed by cowards in 'sheep' clothing.

I remind my kids of their loving aunt Katrina and how strong she was.

I pray that her life wasn't in vain.

Seeking Revenge-Tweet (aka Pammy)

*Can't be mad at the things you've been
through, 'cause they built your muscle
Now you're stronger than you've ever been,
they can't stop your hustle. ~Mary Mary*

There's no doubt in my mind that I was born in the wrong body.

The broads before me have the same thing in common their downfall was a man.

Their daddies, baby daddies, husbands, boyfriends;

But not me that couldn't be me I've never trusted any man.

Because I'm gay always have been, always will be.

I'll never let a man touch me.

It makes me sick.

A man ain't even worthy enough to take out my trash.

My own daddy didn't raise me.

I'm more of a man than he is.

I took care of my mama and my sister.

I've heard and been called it all: dyke, stud, lesbian, fag, bulldagger, carpet muncher, butch, and so much more.

They don't mean anything to me.

I know who I am and how I got like this.

I was about eleven when our white next-door neighbor raped me and stole every part of my femininity.

He was our handyman for the multiplex we stayed in.

My mother had an appointment to be somewhere early that morning and my sister was still asleep.

Our toilet was stopped up and mama said it was okay to let Dale in to fix it then "lock my door and don't open it for nobody".

Dale must have heard my mama start up her car because a few seconds later he was walking in.

I was sitting on the couch in my Tweety Bird pajamas when he walked passed me to fix the toilet.

He mumbled something and continued to the bathroom.

He wasn't in there four whole minutes before he was finished.

I still remember it like it was yesterday.

He was standing over me with his toolbox in one hand and his 'tool' in his other.

I felt a shiver as he leaned down so close to my face that the smell of beer and cigarettes assaulted my nostrils.

I was frozen as he kissed my eleven-year-old lips and licked the sides of my face.

He threatened to play this game with my sister too if I made a sound but even at eleven, I knew that shit wasn't right.

He sat on the couch next to me and stroked my hair as he pulled his pants all the way down.

"Come sit on my lap, gal" those six words are forever tattooed in my mind.

Those six words stole my childhood.

Those six words made me die inside.

When I didn't move, he jerked me by my arm and pulled my size small Tweety Bird pajama pants down and forced himself inside my purity.

I cried as I felt my body rip.

I cried as I bleed out the spot that separated me from the boys in my family.

I remember him digging into my flesh as he invaded my privacy.

I remember never ever wanting to feel this much pain again.

After he was done with me, he pushed me off and made me take a bath while he cleaned up the blood.

I knew then that I would never let a man touch me again.

When my mama got home, I acted as if nothing ever happened.

Something more than rape happened to me that day.

I became mean and callous.

I wouldn't listen to anything my mother told me.

I became a ticking time bomb.

The slightest thing would set me off.

I protected my home, my sister, and mother.

I never let Dale near my sister.

I promised to one day pay him, and I did.

When I turned thirteen, I found my grandfather's gun and I snuck it home.

I hid it from everyone.

I knew my grandfather would blame my uncle.

I never opened my mouth.

I watched Dale for seven months, learned his routine.

I discovered he was raping other girls in the multiplex.

I was waiting for the right moment.

One night I watched from my bedroom window. and I saw him coming back from the corner store.

I made my move.

I was dressed in all black to blend into the darkness.

I crept from behind our building..

I got a clear shot.

I aimed right between his legs and I pulled the trigger.

I missed and it gave him a chance to get closer.

I stumbled a bit because of the recoil, but I was determined to get him.

I closed my eyes and kept shooting until I was out of bullets.

The sound of glass hitting the concrete caused me to open my eyes.

Dale was lying on the ground begging me for help. "ME??

The same one he raped two years and eleven months ago??

ME, the "come sit on my lap, gal?"

I didn't have any bullets left, so I used the butt of the gun to hit him over the head.

The first thud startled me, but I didn't stop until I ended his life by my hands.

I was covered in his dark blood.

I dropped the gun and ran when I heard voices.

People were running to his aid.

They had no idea of the monster I just saved the world from.

On the news, it was reported that a young black boy was seen running from the crime scene.

Reporters and police were going door-to-door looking for the killer.

It was my grandfather's gun that gave me away.

The police came and kicked my mother's door in.

They dragged me away like I was a dog instead of a kid just trying to protect their home.

I stood my ground.

I told them Dale hurt some girls in the multiplex, and I was just trying to save them.

I never mentioned what he did to me.

The other girls denied all my allegations until one of them had a mixed baby.

The girl admitted that Dale raped her and she became pregnant but hid the baby out of fear.

I was given 4 years in a youth detention center.

On my eighteenth birthday, I was released.

By then I had turned so many girls in juvie out.

I was a full-blown stud.

I wear a short haircut.

I tape my titties down.

I keep a bad bitch by my side.

I walk, talk and act the way I should've been born, like a man.

A man caused the demise of Pammy.

She was weak, but Tweet is a strong black man.

Mama's Baby, Daddy's Regret- Christina

*All that I've done wrong, I must have done
something right.
To deserve her love every morning, And
butterfly kisses at night. ~Bob Carlisle*

In the beginning, I never knew what was missing from my life because as they say "you can't miss what you never had".

It was okay that it was just my mama, that's all I needed.

I knew she loved me and I definitely loved her.

I couldn't wait until I was an adult because I would be just like her.

She did what she had to do for the two of us.

I was okay with that because although we never had a lot.

We always had each other.

When I was nine, mama told me she had someone she wanted me to meet.

She dressed me really pretty in a new pink dress with matching sandals.

She combed my long black hair into three beautiful ponytails.

I mean she greased the hell outta my face with Vaseline.

I was shining so much I glowed.

My mother made herself knock out gorgeous.

She also dressed in pink wearing a hip-hugging sundress with her hair cascading around her slim heart shaped face.

She sprayed her "White Diamonds" perfume from her head down to her French manicured toes.

On our way to the restaurant, my mama began to tell me about this special person.

"Baby, I know you've been hearing other little girls talk about their fathers and you've probably wondered if you had one or not.

Well, yes you do have a father and that's whom you will meet today.

His name is Reginald.

He loves you so much and can't wait to meet you.

As we pulled into the parking lot of the restaurant, my mother checked the mirror to make sure there wasn't a single hair out of place.

Her face was flawless.

She threw on her favorite pair of sunglasses and straightened my dress as we walked through the door.

Reginald was standing next to a booth in the back of the diner.

He looked like me.

He was tall with smooth brown skin, very muscular or maybe it was the tightness of his black Adidas tracksuit.

He rushed to me lifting me off my feet and spinning me in the air causing me to be dizzy when he sat me back on my feet.

I looked up at my mother, although, she had on sunglasses I could still see the tears streaming down her face.

She gave me a reassuring nod that everything was okay.

Reginald kneeled down in front of me and smiled saying "Hi, I'm your dad.

I really missed you and I thought about you every day I was locked..."

My mother cut him off, "She doesn't know anything about that.

Let's just sit down and order her some food.

Doesn't she look beautiful?"

After that first meeting, everything changed for us.

We lived better than we ever had before.

My daddy was giving mama money for me.

I got a new bed and even a television in my room and all new furniture in the whole house.

This only lasted for six years.

He was back in jail by the time I was fourteen.

This time my mother and I moved to Georgia because my father had multiple women and kids with added drama.

Years had passed, and I received letters and collect calls, from the man I knew as Reggie, with broken promises to make it up to me when he gets released because he changed and is ready to settle down with my mama.

I didn't know what all of this meant.

Until one day, I got this package in the mail for Christmas.

It was a box loaded with name brand clothes, Nikes, a starter coat, herringbone chain, and gold hoop earrings.

All of these things were things my mother couldn't afford to buy me; my dad was providing from jail.

I was bought that quickly.

My daddy won me over with material affection.

Little did I know, that would be my downfall.

Every guy I dated after that showed me love by the things they bought.

I became so materialistic.

If you couldn't buy the biggest or baddest purses, shoes, and clothes, then I wouldn't give you the time of day.

When I was twenty-one, my boyfriend bought me my first brand new car.

He treated me like crap but his "I'm sorry," gifts were the *bomb.com.*

I mean, he didn't hit me but he grabbed my hair and held me up against the wall a few times.

I would leave for a day or two, but I was greeted with a shopping spree in Miami when I came back.

I left him when he ran out of money and I wrecked the car.

I know what you think, that I'm a gold digger right?

Wrong.

I'm just my daddy's daughter.

I thought money from a man equated with love.

I searched pockets and banks for affections.

At age twenty-six, with a baby coming, I realized I had to be more reliable and stable.

My father was released from federal prison, and I finally met my siblings.

He brought all of them to my baby shower.

They all came bearing so many gifts that I didn't have to open the gifts from my other guests.

My father was back in my life but for how long?

Had he had enough of the fast money lifestyle?

I wasn't getting younger and paper chasing would be harder with an extra mouth to feed.

My mama's warning of "don't let money buy your self-respect," was finally starting to sink in as my stomach start to expand.

She was the only constant thing in my life before I had my son.

I finally found real love from a man for the first time in my life.

Evan and I were getting married and I had made peace with the woman I use to be compared to who I am now.

I no longer need to be validated by my father, or any other man.

I was feeling the love from this man and my son.

Two months after I had my son, Reggie wound up back in jail under the RICO ACT.

He wrote me a letter apologizing for not being the man I needed him to be (I'm sure this was something my mother made him say).

He asked me what I wanted from him and I wrote back "You were all I ever wanted and needed."

Those were the only eight words in the whole letter.

During the planning of my wedding, Reggie was still incarcerated.

After six months of coming up empty and having no real evidence to convict him.

He was finally released exactly two days before I was changing my last name.

The night before my wedding, Reggie called me at four o'clock in the morning asking for directions to my wedding venue.

I was still asleep and it wasn't clear but I heard him ask me, "Can I walk you down the aisle?"

I talked it over with my mother and my uncle and we agreed.

It was MY one special day and the choice was mine to make.

Nobody should get in their feelings with the decision I make.

After much thought and consideration and a crying phone session with Evan, we decided that my uncle James should be the one to give me away.

I wasn't sure how the day would end since it started out rough.

My wedding was everything I thought it would be, even with a crying baby.

While we were saying our vows, RJ started crying uncontrollably and just when I was about to ask for him, Reggie got up and took him from my mother and walked out with him.

I was so relieved.

When it was time to take pictures my dad brought a sleeping RJ to be included.

He turned to walk away; I said,

"Daddy, where are you going? I want my whole family in our wedding photos."

The smile on his face was priceless and at that point, I was *"daddy's girl."*

Looking back on that day, I couldn't have made a better choice.

My father passed away in 2008, but I had that one day when everything was perfect for a moment at least.

We spent his last few months together.

I was right there when he took his last breath and made a lot of deathbed confessions and apologies.

My siblings that knew Reggie better planned his funeral, but they included me every step of the way.

I still read all the letters that he wrote me while he was locked away.

I will give them to RJ one day, so he will know the strength he comes from.

Releasing- Free

I believe in dreams again
I believe that love will never end
And like the river finds the sea
I was lost now I'm free ~ Whitney Houston

You think you know me you don't

But you really don't.

You know the more I think about it, I'm really YOU.

I'm every woman that has ever been hurt.

I saw babies and mothers lives taken and I couldn't save them all.

I was told to pray for them.

I did.

I asked God for peace and understanding.

I found myself questioning more than I was praying.

I've watched my people be killed and destroyed and I couldn't fix it.

I've witnessed rape and abuse.

Hell, I've been raped and abused, lied on and cheated on.

I've been beaten within inches of being dead.

All these external conflicts affected me internally.

I was LIFE, BABY and I was taken for granted.

I was so hurt from the name-calling, neglect, and abuse.

I felt as though I couldn't take any more.

I was dead on the inside.

I was a shell of the woman torn and scorned.

A damn good-looking woman is what I appeared to be on the outside.

I'm a dime and any man should be lucky if I give him the time of day.

I kept my appearance up because I had to.

Nails and hair were done.

I dressed to the nines with nowhere to go.

I cried myself to sleep so many nights.

I searched for answers; nothing.

I prayed for peace; none.

I sought out friends.

No one was around.

I fed in the negative stigma that had been placed on my life years ago.

I was weak minded.

I didn't know it.

I thought because I had nice things and a little money in the bank I was okay.

None of that was doing me any good anyhow.

I stop eating and sleeping even stopped praying.

Then one night it all turned bad.

The pressure was too much.

I begged for death.

I called my mama, and she didn't answer.

I called my best friend, and she was too busy with her kids.

I called my sister, and she was sexing her new husband.

I called my pastor, and he was visiting elderly members at the hospital.

I called my coworker that I go to lunch with, and she was on a conference call.

I needed someone, anyone, but found no one.

I cried out for relief, for the pain to stop.

I walked to the bathroom cabinet pulled and out the bottle of Xanax the doctor gave me last month for my anxiety attacks.

I'd never taken them.

I poured a glass of wine, emptied the pills in my hand, and tossed them into my mouth and picked up the wine and turned it up.

One glass wasn't big enough.

Two handfuls and the bottle was consumed.

Finally, I can get some peace.

I walked back to my office and pulled out my old photo albums.

I decided to write letters to my mother, sister, and friends.

I want to let them know what I'm feeling and why.

After the second letter, my eyes start to feel heavy and my soul feels lighter.

I see a light with a warm glow and I can hear a sweet song.

I think it is "Amazing Grace".

I close my eyes as I recite the Lord's Prayer and lay back on the couch.

I see the sweetest faces and smiles with welcoming arms.

I am at peace.

I am home.

I am Free.

Ways to Support Your Sister

I once heard someone quote, "It doesn't dim your light any to help your fellow sister shine." Don't tear each other down.

Be silent and let God show you how to support others.

Think about how many labels you have on (shoes, purses, shirts, pants etc.), how can you support so many strangers and not help your neighbor?

Look around you, how many of your girlfriends are starting new businesses that you can patronize with? Buy her cake, use her catering company, and support startups.

Do you at least try to be friendly?

Is there a younger girl that attends your church? Take a chance on her and get to know her. She may be going through a tough time and just needs your expertise on cooking, cleaning, or motherhood.

Please visit my website for more information and resources. www.Shastamignon.com

Join our private Facebook community: **The Weight She Carried Together**. It's a place where members can connect, continue the discussion on the topics discussed in the book, as well get more information on upcoming events based off the book.